Kindergarten Scholar Contents

Math

Identifying Geometric Shapes	2
Counting	8
Counting	11
Patterns	14
Identifying Geometric Shapes	16
Picture Graphs	21
Patterns/Counting	24
Counting	26
Comparing Numbers	29
Penny, Nickel, Dime, Quarter	34
Counting	39
Number Sequence	42
Graphs	44
Half and Whole	48
Measurement	49
Patterns	51
Telling Time	53

Basic Skills

Identifying Colors	6
Likenesses and Differences	7
Colors	10
Matching Like Items	15
Comparing Sizes	17
Identifying Opposites	28
Eye-Hand Coordination	37
Matching Colors	38
Visual Discrimination	47
Visual Discrimination	54
Drawing	56

Social Studies

Maps	4
Name, Address, Telephone Number	19
Present and Past	22

Science

Animal Babies	9
Emotions	27
Food Groups	30
Food Groups	31
Recycling	33
Colors in a Rainbow	50
The Senses	52

Language Arts

Rhyming Words	12
Story Order	18
Alphabet and Beginning Sounds	20
Alphabet and Beginning Sounds	23
Alphabet and Beginning Sounds	32
Alphabet and Beginning Sounds	35
Rhyming Words	36
Word Meanings	40
Prepositions	41
Alphabet and Beginning Sounds	43
Alphabetical Order	46

And More...

Summer Scholar, Grade K	57
Activities to Share	112
Recommended Reading	118
Answers	120

Off to the fair!

Look for ◯s along the way. Color them 🖍.

Look for ☐s, too. Color them 🖍.

Try it!

Get out your crayons, a sheet of paper, and some cans, milk bottle caps, or cups. Trace around the bottoms to make circles of different colors all over the paper. Create a pretty design.

September 30th

A square is a shape that has four sides. All the sides are the same length.

©School Zone Publishing Company

3

Math: Identifying Geometric Shapes

Where can we go?

Start at the .

Draw a  line.

Go past the .

Follow the path to the .

MAP KEY

Entrance

Picnic Area

Midway Games

Animal Barns

Pioneer Exhibit

Pet Show Ring

Rides

Food Tent

A map is a kind of picture that helps you figure out what way to go. A **map key** helps you read the small pictures, or **symbols**, on a map.

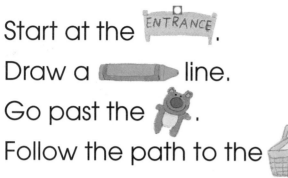

Social Studies: Maps

＿Try it! ＿

Use blocks to build a map of the fair. Create a way to go in, paths to follow, and lots of fun things to do. Drive a toy or truck with toy people and animals. Have a great time!

Social Studies: Maps

Look! Balloons!

Draw a —— from each crayon to the balloon that is the same color.

red

blue

yellow

green

orange

purple

Try it!

Which color is your favorite? Find three things that are that color. Draw a picture of them with your favorite color marker.

6

Pick a balloon

X the balloon in each row that's different.

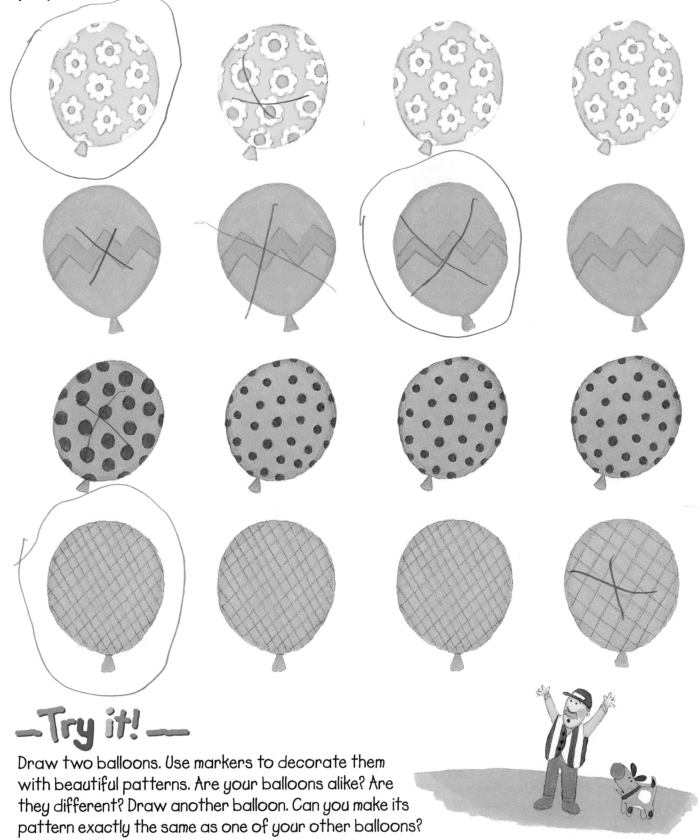

—Try it!—

Draw two balloons. Use markers to decorate them with beautiful patterns. Are your balloons alike? Are they different? Draw another balloon. Can you make its pattern exactly the same as one of your other balloons?

7

Sheep pens

Let's peek in.

How many sheep do you see?

◯ the right number.

1 ② 3

1 2 ③

① 2 3

1 2 ③

─Try it!─

You can do finger addition. Hold up three fingers on one hand. Now hold up three on the other. How many fingers are up? Try this again using different numbers of fingers.

8

Math: Counting

Feathered friends

Count the eggs.

Write the numbers or make tally marks.

◯ the nest that has the most eggs.

3

4   4

2

5

–Try it!–

Ask an adult to help you make this eggs-ellent treat. Melt one teaspoon of butter in a skillet. Cut a three-inch hole in the center of a slice of bread. Brown one side of the bread in the skillet, turn the bread over, and break an egg into the hole. Cover the pan and cook for three minutes. Yum!

Math: Counting

Silly costume parade

Listen for rhyming words as you read about the parade.

I see a  in a .

I see a in a .

I see s in s.

—Try it!—

Scarves, neckties, and hats—either old ones you have around the house or some you buy at a thrift store—make great costumes. You can make believe you're a pirate, a ballerina, an astronaut, or a race car driver.

I see a 🐐 in a 🧥.

I see a 🦊 in 🧦s.

I see 🐱 🐱s.

Draw what the 🐱 🐱s are wearing.

What did the bear wear in the parade?
Nothing. It was bare!

13

Language Arts: Rhyming Words

Rows of clothes

The clothes make color patterns.
Color the last picture to finish each pattern.
Make your own color pattern in the last row.

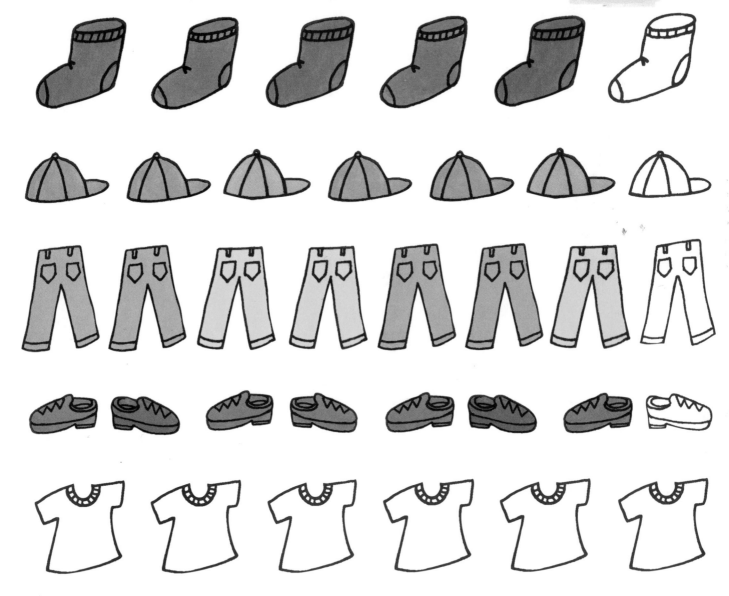

_Try it! —

It's fun to make sound patterns. You can slap your legs and clap
your hands to make a pattern that sounds like this: slap/clap,
slap/clap, slap/clap. Or you can stamp your feet and say toot-
toot stamp/toot-toot stamp. What other sound patterns can
you make? Have a friend copy your sound patterns.

14

Math: Patterns

What a mess!

Let's help pick them up.

Draw a —— to show the ones that match.

—Try it!—

Next time a load of wash is done, help sort the socks into pairs. Someone will thank you!

Why did Wags wear orange socks?
Because his purple ones were in the wash!

Basic Skills: Matching Like Items

Look! A path!

Follow the ◯s.

Color them ▬▬.

Where do they lead?

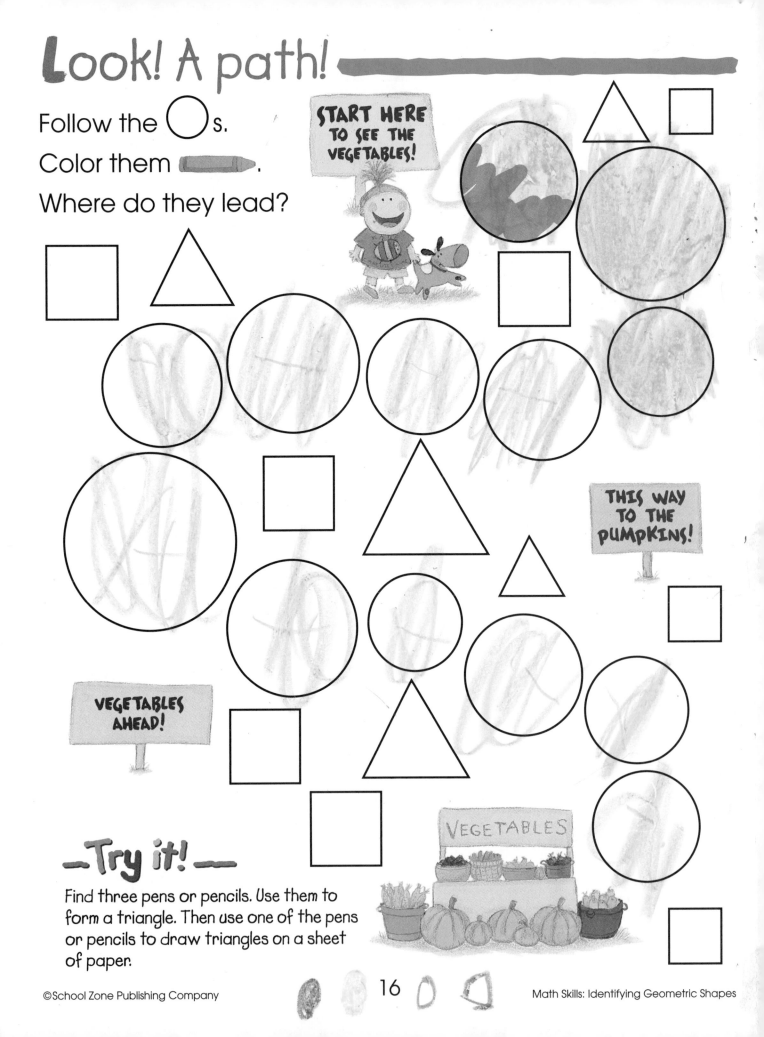

START HERE TO SEE THE VEGETABLES!

THIS WAY TO THE PUMPKINS!

VEGETABLES AHEAD!

VEGETABLES

—Try it!—

Find three pens or pencils. Use them to form a triangle. Then use one of the pens or pencils to draw triangles on a sheet of paper.

16

Math Skills: Identifying Geometric Shapes

Your favorite fruit

The students are having a fruit party.
What did they bring? Answer the questions.

7				7
6				6
5				5
4				4
3				3
2				2
1				1

Try it!

Ask your family and friends
what fruit they like best.
Make a graph to show the
fruit most people like.

How many 🍐s?   3   6   2   ④

How many 🍌s?   ⑦   4   3   5

How many 🍊s?   ⑥   3   5   7

How many 🍎s?   4   6   2   ⑤

21

Math: Picture Graphs

It's a Pioneer Village

Everyone here does what people did long ago.

Well, almost everyone...

✗ things that don't belong in this long-ago scene.

—Try it!—

Look around your house. What do you see that would not have been in a house long ago? Would people have used something else instead? What would they have used?

22

What did you see?

Here are some things you saw in Pioneer Village.

What letter begins each picture name?

◯ the capital and lowercase letters.

Ee   E   e   C

Ff   d   f   F

Gg   G   b   g

Hh   b   H   h

What side of a goose has
the most feathers?

The outside!

–Try it!–

Divide a sheet of paper into four boxes. Write **Ee** in one section,
Ff in another, and **Gg** and **Hh** in the others. In each section,
draw a picture of something that begins with that letter.

23

Language Arts: Alphabet and Beginning Sounds

Counting at Pioneer Village

Draw the next one in each row.

—Try it! —

Count the pictures again. This time count by twos:
2, 4, 6, 8. Try counting your toy cars, your books, even
your french fries by twos.

24

Math: Patterns/Counting

Two, four, six, eight,
Who do we appreciate?
Wags, Wags,
Hooray! Hooray!

25

Math: Patterns/Counting

Let's ride!

Hooray! Each of us has a ticket for three rides.

✓ your favorite ride.

Then count the people. How many in all?_____

Try it!

Have you ever been on a ride? What was it like? Draw
a picture of the ride and tell someone about it.

26

Math: Counting

Cleanup time

Draw ——s to put the items in the correct recycle bins.

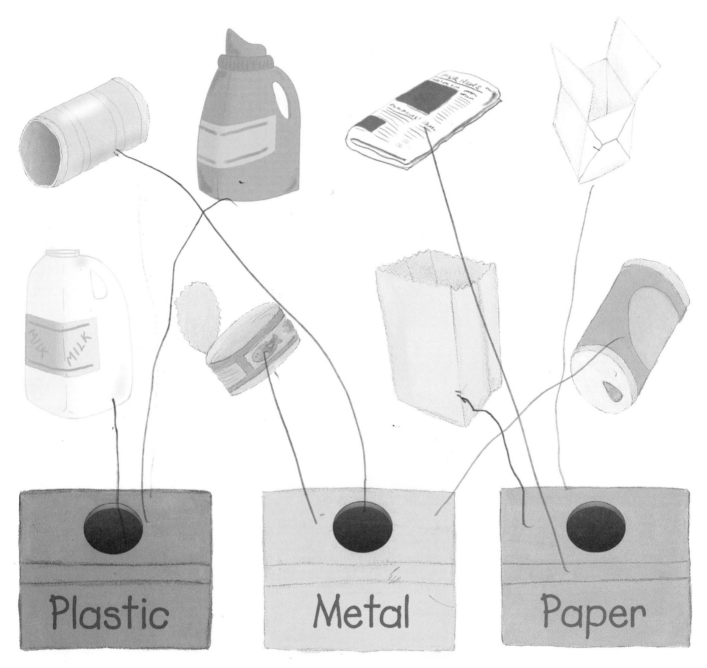

Plastic

Metal

Paper

—Try it!—

Here's a way to recycle soft-drink cans. Wash them out and use them as blocks. You can stack them to make towers or line them up to build walls. What else can you do with the cans?

33

At the gift shop

How much do the gifts cost?
Draw a — from the coins to the gifts.

STICKERS
5¢

TOY
ANIMALS
10¢

PENNY
CANDY
1¢

POSTCARDS
25¢

FAIR

FAIR

FAIR

1¢

5¢

10¢

25¢

—Try it!—

What would you like to buy at the gift shop? Collect some
pennies. Count the number of pennies you need to buy the
item you want. Then pick a gift for a friend and count the
pennies you need to buy it.

34

Math: Penny, Nickel, Dime, Quarter

Where is Lilly?

Oh, dear! Lilly is lost. Help her find Ms. Liz.
Draw a — along the path she must take.

—Try it!—

What would you do if you got lost in a store?
Talk with your family about it. Make a plan so
you'll know what to do if you get lost.

Basic Skills: Eye-Hand Coordination

Time for a treat

Find crayons that match the colors of the dots.
Color the shapes to discover what the treat is.

_Try it! _

Ask an adult to help you make a cold dessert. Mix one 14-ounce
can of sweetened condensed milk, 2/3 cup chocolate syrup, and
two cups heavy cream, whipped. Stir the ingredients together
and pour them into a foil-lined loaf pan. Freeze for six hours.
Remove from pan. Peel off the foil, slice, and enjoy!

38

We like ice cream!

◯ the number of servings in each row.
Color the ice cream.

1 2 ③ 4 5

1 2 3 ④ 5

1 ② 3 4 5

1 2 3 4 ⑤

─Try it!─

What's your favorite ice
cream treat? Draw it.

You scream,
I scream,
We all scream,
For ice cream!

yay!   Yay!
    yay!

39

Look at the games!

What are the kids doing?
Use words that tell where.

1. How many ⚾s are **high**? ___3___

2. How many ⚾s are **low**? ___2___

—Try it!—

It's easy to make sentences. Start by saying a name such as Lilly. Then say an action word: **jumps**. Put the two words together and you have a sentence: **Lilly jumps**. Now make up more sentences. Remember, every sentence has a naming word and an action word.

Language Arts: Word Meanings

3. How many s are **inside** the tent? _4_ 4

4. How many s are **outside** the tent? _3_ 3

5. How many s are jumping **over**? _2_ 2

Language Arts: Prepositions

Missing numbers

Write each missing number.

©School Zone Publishing Company

42

Math: Number Sequence

Try it!

To do this, you'll need a marker and ten sheets of paper. Trace around your foot on each sheet. Write a number from one to ten on each foot. Then lay out the sheets in order. Can you walk ten "feet"?

That's Wags doing an imitation of a duck!

Get it? He's ducking!

Lots of prizes

What letter begins each picture name?
◯ the capital and lowercase letters.

Uu	u	j	U
Vv	L	V	V
Ww	W	k	w
Xx	x	m	X
Yy	z	Y	y
Zz	Z	Z	Q

— Try it! —

Make up an alphabet game. Write the letters of the alphabet on a sheet of paper for an indoor game or with chalk on the sidewalk for an outdoor game. Throw a button at the letters. Name the letter on which it lands. Then think of a word that begins with that letter.

Language Arts: Alphabet and Beginning Sounds

Your favorite

What is the most popular ride at the fair?
Color one box for each person on a ride.

3 5 7 4

Try it!

Ask your family and friends what ride
they like best. Make a graph to show
the rides people like.

Math: Graphs

45

What is it?

Follow the dots from **A** to **Z** and you'll find out.

—Try it! —

You may not be able to juggle, but with some practice you can bounce
a ball and catch it. Here's a rhyme to say as you bounce:

 ABCs and vegetable goop.
 What will I find in the alphabet soup?
 A, B, C, D, E . . .

Name a funny word that starts with the letter on which you miss.
This game is fun to play with a friend.

Language Arts: Alphabetical Order

Clowns in a row

Let's measure each clown. Use a .
How many s tall is each one?

1._____ 2._____ 3._____ 4._____

⎯Try it!⎯

Measure some of your toys. How many pennies long are
your toy cars? How high is this book? What else can you
use to measure? You might try using your feet, a block, or
even your whole body to measure something big like a rug.

Math: Measurement

Hooray! The sun!

There's a rainbow in the sky.
Read these color words.
Color the rainbow.

red   orange   yellow   green   blue   indigo   violet

—Try it! —

Get out your watercolors, a paintbrush, and a sheet of white paper.
Experiment with blending colors. Mix red and yellow to get orange
and red and blue to make purple. Mix blue and yellow and what do
you get? Paint a pretty picture with your colors.

Everybody looks! CHRISTIANA

Color the flowers to finish the patterns.

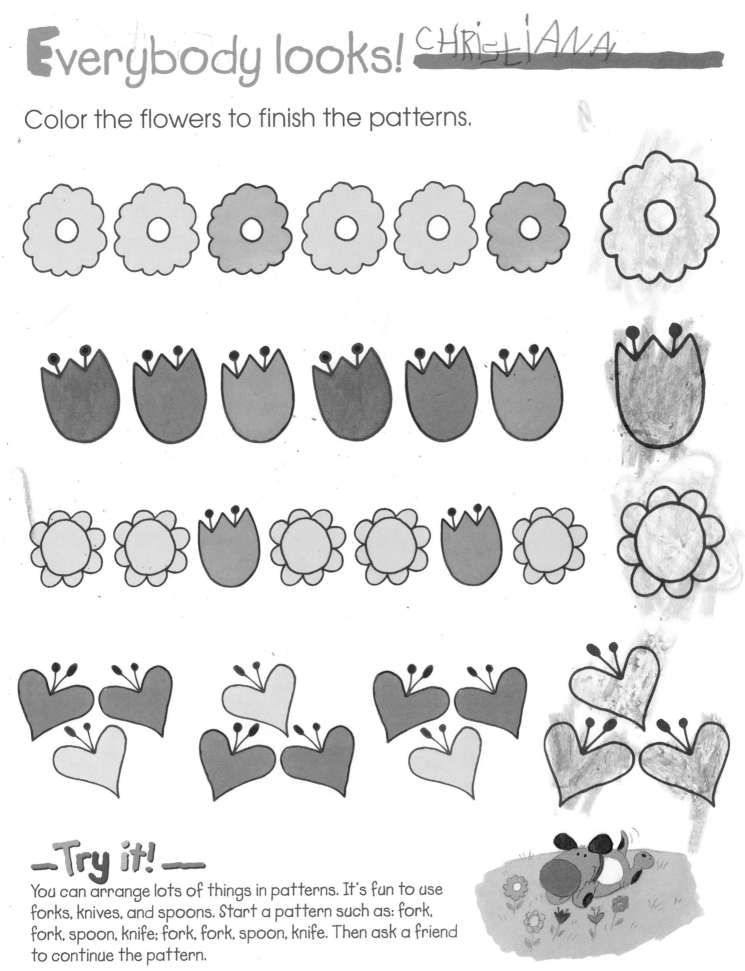

—Try it! —

You can arrange lots of things in patterns. It's fun to use forks, knives, and spoons. Start a pattern such as: fork, fork, spoon, knife; fork, fork, spoon, knife. Then ask a friend to continue the pattern.

51

Math: Patterns

Smell with your nose Christiana

The children are using their five senses.
They are seeing, hearing, smelling, tasting, and touching.
Draw ——s to the sign. Show the sense each is using.

—Try it!—

Tell someone everything Sam can do. Use this sentence
pattern: Sam can _____ with his _____. You might
say, for example, Sam can feel raindrops with his hand.

Science: The Senses

Time to go home CHRISTIANA

Do you remember all the things we did today?
Write 1, 2, 3, and 4 to show the order.

-Try it!-

Make a practice clock. You'll need a paper plate, two thin strips of
heavy paper for the hands, and a brad to hold the hands in the center.
Write the numbers from 1 to 12 around the clock. Then move the hands
to make the clock show the same times as the clocks on this page.

53

Math: Telling Time

We'll remember

Lots of things we saw are hidden in this picture.

Try it!

Name seven more things you remember from the fair.
It's OK to look through the book again for help.

these in the picture.

Basic Skills: Visual Discrimination

My favorite

What did you like best about the fair?
Draw a picture of it here.
Then tell someone about your picture.

Which joke was your favorite?

56

Basic Skills: Drawing

H_2O

Cc

Summer Scholar
Contents

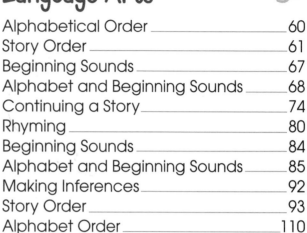

1234

Basic Skills

Visual Discrimination ⎯⎯⎯ 58
Following Directions ⎯⎯⎯ 62
Visual Discrimination ⎯⎯⎯ 65
Same or Different ⎯⎯⎯ 71
Classifying ⎯⎯⎯ 72
Eye-Hand Coordination ⎯⎯⎯ 81
Opposites ⎯⎯⎯ 89
Eye-Hand Coordination ⎯⎯⎯ 94
Drawing ⎯⎯⎯ 97
Same or Different ⎯⎯⎯ 99
Matching ⎯⎯⎯ 102
Things That Go Together ⎯⎯⎯ 104
Size Relationship ⎯⎯⎯ 105
Color Words ⎯⎯⎯ 106
Things That Go Together ⎯⎯⎯ 108

Math

Patterns ⎯⎯⎯ 59
Money ⎯⎯⎯ 66
Classifying ⎯⎯⎯ 69
Graphing ⎯⎯⎯ 70
Patterns ⎯⎯⎯ 73
Counting ⎯⎯⎯ 75
Counting ⎯⎯⎯ 78
Graphing ⎯⎯⎯ 79
Estimating ⎯⎯⎯ 86
Geometric Shapes ⎯⎯⎯ 88
Telling Time ⎯⎯⎯ 90
Counting ⎯⎯⎯ 91
Number Recognition ⎯⎯⎯ 109

Language Arts

Alphabetical Order ⎯⎯⎯ 60
Story Order ⎯⎯⎯ 61
Beginning Sounds ⎯⎯⎯ 67
Alphabet and Beginning Sounds ⎯⎯⎯ 68
Continuing a Story ⎯⎯⎯ 74
Rhyming ⎯⎯⎯ 80
Beginning Sounds ⎯⎯⎯ 84
Alphabet and Beginning Sounds ⎯⎯⎯ 85
Making Inferences ⎯⎯⎯ 92
Story Order ⎯⎯⎯ 93
Alphabet Order ⎯⎯⎯ 110

Social Studies

Name, Address, Telephone Number ⎯⎯⎯ 87
Likes and Dislikes ⎯⎯⎯ 96
Families ⎯⎯⎯ 100
Families ⎯⎯⎯ 101
Citizenship ⎯⎯⎯ 103

Science

The Senses ⎯⎯⎯ 64
Animal Babies ⎯⎯⎯ 76
Life Cycles ⎯⎯⎯ 77
Emotions ⎯⎯⎯ 82
Recycling ⎯⎯⎯ 83
Weather ⎯⎯⎯ 95
Food Groups ⎯⎯⎯ 98

And More...

Activities to Share ⎯⎯⎯ 112
Recommended Reading ⎯⎯⎯ 118
Answers ⎯⎯⎯ 120

Where do you put a noisy dog?
In a barking lot!

Circle the things that are silly.

How many silly things did you find? ___6___

Make up a silly story using bandage puppets. Draw faces on the pad part of several finger bandages. Then put the bandages on your fingers and make up a funny conversation.

Visual Discrimination

Beach Beauties

What gets wetter
the more it dries?
A towel!

The children are ready to dry off.

Draw a line to help them find their towels.

Make a pattern trail of sticky notes on a table, on a wall, or even on the floor! Use two or three colors of small sticky notes and see how far you can make your pattern go!

Connect the dots from A to M. Color the picture.

Create an alphabet collage. Cut out bright and colorful letters from an old magazine. Paste the letters on a piece of construction paper and make a design out of them.

What happens first? What happens next?

Number the pictures in 1, 2, 3, 4 order.

Make up a story about the four pictures. Tell what happens in each picture in order. Then try making up a new story by talking about each picture in a different order!

Off to the Zoo with You!

Draw a line to help the children get to the Zoo.

Go to the ▬ .

Turn and go to the ▲ .

Turn and go to the ■ .

Go straight to

©School Zone Publishing Company

Following Directions

Knock Knock. Who's there?
Ocelot. Ocelot who?
Ocelot of questions, don't you?

THE
ZOO

MOVIES

Draw a chalk trail outside on the ground leading from one
place to another. Then try different ways to follow the trail.
Hop along it, walk along it, skip along it, or tiptoe along it.

63

Following Directions

Taste, touch, smell, hear, and see.
Mouth, hands, nose, ears, eyes... Me!

Which things can you smell?

Which can you see? taste? touch? hear?

Color in the boxes that show the senses you use.

Go on a listening walk. Walk very quietly through your home or outside with an adult. Listen very carefully as you go. How many different sounds can you hear? Can you see what is making each sound? Can you imitate the sounds you hear?

The Senses

Can You Find It?

Did you know that hippopotami can't swim or that crocodiles can't chew?

What can you find in the picture?

Draw a line to each thing in the picture.

Play "I Spy" with a parent or friend. Look around you and find something to "spy." Describe three things about it. Can your friend figure out what you saw? Now ask your friend to describe something for you to find.

Visual Discrimination

What did one penny say
to the other penny?
Together we make cents!

Draw a line to the coin you will need to buy each treat.

GREAT JOB!!

Did you ever make a coin rubbing? Tape a penny, nickel, dime, or quarter to a piece of white paper. Now color the paper with a pencil or crayon. What do you see?

Circle the things that start with **b**.

How many can you find? __6 6__ Good Job

Look around you. Can you find something that starts with the letter **b**? Draw a picture of what you see.

Beginning Sounds

Circle the picture that begins with the same sound.

A + ⭐

Aa Kk Mm Pp Rr Tt

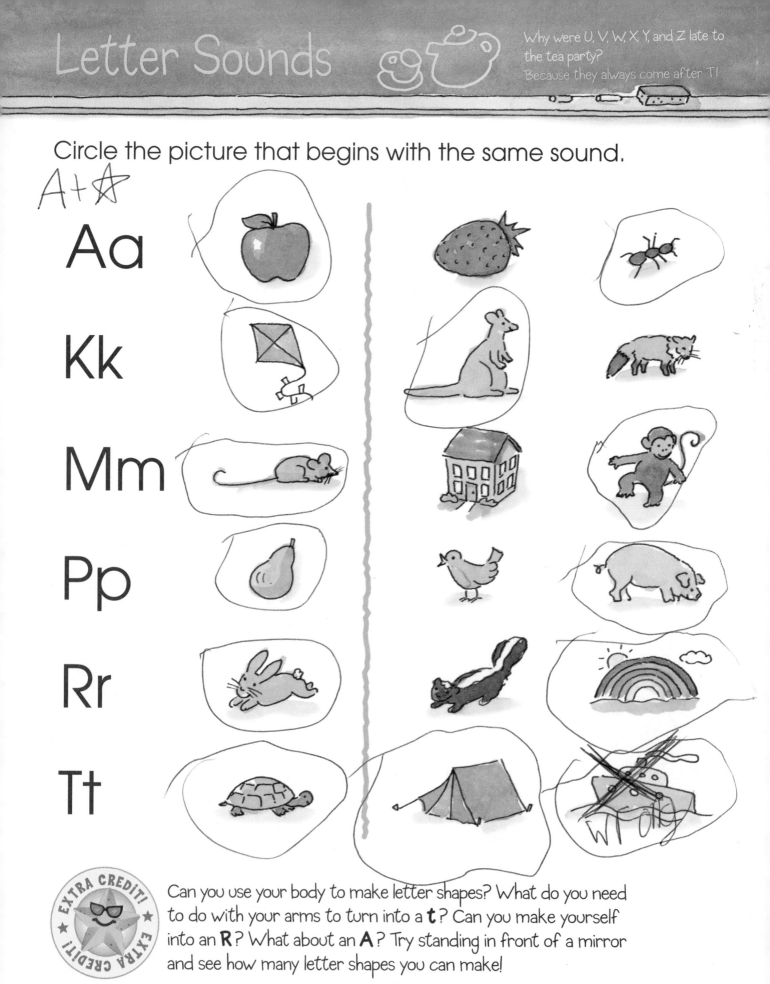

Can you use your body to make letter shapes? What do you need to do with your arms to turn into a **t**? Can you make yourself into an **R**? What about an **A**? Try standing in front of a mirror and see how many letter shapes you can make!

EXTRA CREDIT! EXTRA CREDIT!

68

Animals of All Kinds

Look at the animals. Then answer the questions.

1. How many have four feet? ___4___

2. How many have spots? ___3___ 3

3. How many have spots and also four feet? ___1___

You can use an empty egg carton as a container for sorting a variety of things. Sort buttons, rocks, old keys, or nature objects you gathered on an outside walk. Choose your own categories and use one section for each kind of thing.

Classifying

Collecting Seashells

What kinds of shells did the children collect?

Fill in the graph to show how many of each.

	1	2	3	4	5	6	7	8
🐚	✓	✓		altgether ✓				
🐚	✓	✓	✓			all together ✓		
🐚	✗	✓	✓ ✓					all together ✓

Can you find another way to sort the shells? What groups would you choose? Which group would have the most shells? Which group would have the least?

Try to say this tongue twister quickly three times in a row: She sells seashells down by the seashore.

Circle the seashell in each row that is different.

Play an estimating game with rocks, pebbles, buttons, or paper clips. Gather your estimating material. Grab a small handful in each hand. Put the two piles on a table. Which do you think has more? Count each pile to check your guess.

EXTRA CREDIT! EXTRA CREDIT! EXTRA CREDIT!

Same or Different

Same or Different?

Summer hats are fun.
They shade eyes from the sun.
Winter hats are warm
In wind and snow and storm.

In each row there is one thing that does not belong.

Can you circle it?

EXTRA CREDIT! ★ EXTRA CREDIT!

Make a summer sun hat. 1.) Decorate a sheet of newspaper and place it on top of your head. 2.) Hold down the middle of the paper. 3.) Use masking tape to form a brim. 4.) Trim the brim into a circle. Glue ribbon, feathers, and other decorations to your sun hat.

What Comes Next?

Knock Knock. Who's there?
Lettuce. Lettuce who?
Lettuce in the pool! It's hot today!

Finish each color pattern.

EXTRA CREDIT! EXTRA CREDIT

Can you make up your own sound pattern using claps, snaps, and stamps? Challenge a friend to listen to your pattern and repeat it!

Patterns

If you throw a white rock into a green pond what happens to the rock? It gets wet!

Look at the three pictures.

Draw a picture of what you think happens next.

Make stick puppets. Cut out pictures of people or animals from old magazines and glue them onto ice cream sticks or chopsticks. When the glue dries, use the puppets to tell your own stories.

Who has two feet? Who has four feet? Who has more feet?

Count the animals and people. Write the number in the boxes.

Two feet
> Girl
> DUCK
> Bird

Four feet
> Bunny
> Dog

More feet
> Buterfly

There are more of which animal?

There are fewer of which animal?

EXTRA CREDIT!
Can you figure out how many feet live at your home? Count the feet of all the people and animals that live at your home! How many hands live at your home? Is there the same number of hands as feet?

Whose Baby Is Whose?

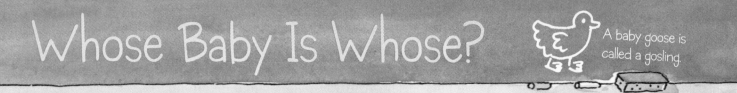

A baby goose is called a gosling.

Draw lines from the baby animals to their mothers.

EXTRA CREDIT! ★ EXTRA CREDIT

Make a picture of a goose from a hand tracing. Place your hand on a piece of paper and trace around it using a crayon or marker. Now draw a head on the top of your thumb and draw two legs and feet on the bottom of your hand.

76

Animal Babies

How They Grow...

Write 1, 2, and 3 to show the order.

Plant a lima bean seed in a can filled with dirt. Set it in a window and water it every day, just enough to keep the soil moist. Pretty soon you will see your seed turn into a seedling and then a plant!

By the Pond

Count how many.

frogs    (4)   1   3

ducks   6   (5)   4

mice   (3)   4   2

butterflies   2   (5)   (4)

children   3   6   (5)

123
321
One, two, three. Come outside with me!
Three, two, one. Let's play in the sun!

Color one box for each animal or person.

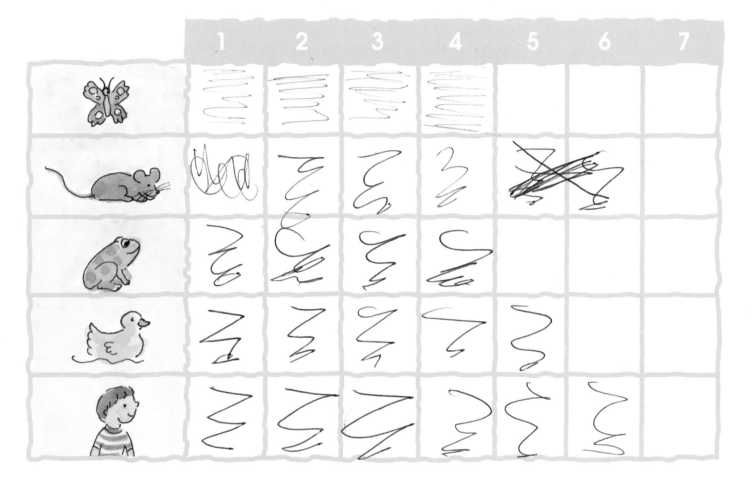

	1	2	3	4	5	6	7
butterfly	✓	✓	✓	✓			
mouse	✓	✓	✓	✓	✓		
frog	✓	✓	✓	✓			
duck	✓	✓	✓	✓	✓		
boy	✓	✓	✓	✓	✓	✓	

There are most of what? Circle.

Make a counting collection! Gather 10 paper plates. Use a marker to label the plates with the numbers 1-10. Then gather up different kinds of items to display on each plate. Match the number of items to the number on each plate.

Mishy fishy, omy gishy
Washy wooshy, itsy gooshy.

Circle the picture that rhymes with the first one.

EXTRA CREDIT! EXTRA CREDIT! EXTRA CREDIT!

Try making up silly rhymes using nonsense words!

Litsy fitsy wampa woo!   Mitsy bitsy honka hoo!

80

Rhyming

Let's Go Fishing!

Knock Knock. Who's there?
Aardvark. Aardvark who?
Aardvark a hundred miles for one of your smiles.

Draw a line to get to the pond.

There are lots of things to see at a pond. The next
time you go to a pond, count the number of bugs, fish,
and animals you see.

81

Eye-Hand Coordination

Knock Knock. Who's there?
Howie. Howie who?
I'm fine. How are you?

What face would you make? Circle one or both.

happy   sad

sad   angry

scared   sad

sad   happy

EXTRA CREDIT! EXTRA CREDIT!

Make up a story to go with the picture.
How does your story start? What happens
in the middle? How does it end?

Emotions

Recycle!

Knock Knock. Who's there?
Juicy. Juicy who?
Juicy what I saw?

Help the family clean up after their picnic.

Draw a line to show where to recycle each item.

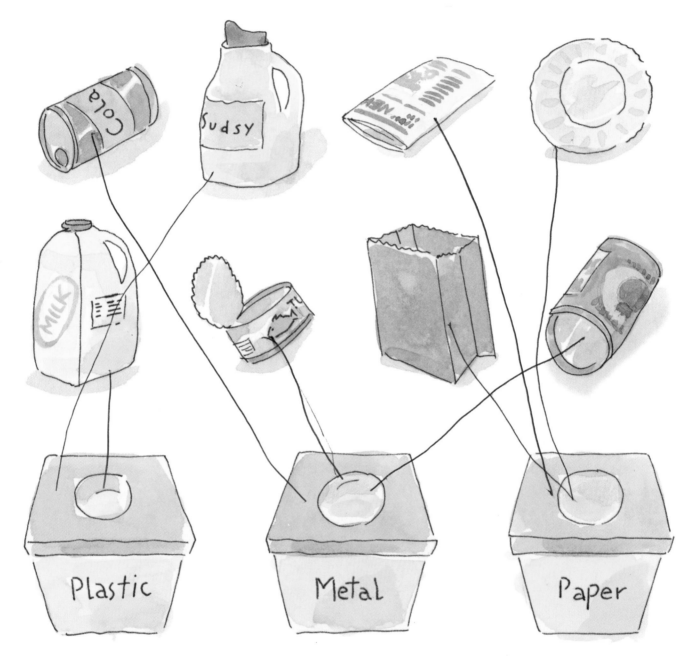

Plastic   Metal   Paper

EXTRA CREDIT! EXTRA CREDIT!

Find new uses for old recyclables. Turn an old cardboard tube into a kazoo. Use a rubber band and a piece of wax paper to cover one end of a cardboard tube. Now hum, sing, or talk through the other end. It's a kazoo!

Recycling

Zoo Animals

Did you know that a baby giraffe stands 6 feet tall on the day it is born?

Write the letter that begins the name of each animal.

Ape

la
oz

owl

Zebra

Lion

Beginning Sounds

Ice! Ice! Ice!
In fruit juice
Ice is nice!

Here are things to take on a picnic.

Circle the matching letters.

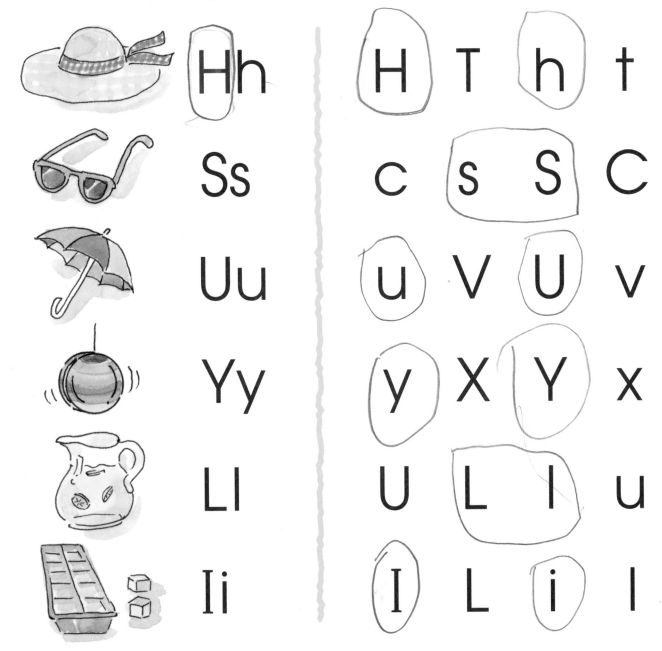

Hh   H T h t

Ss   c s S C

Uu   u V U v

Yy   y X Y x

Ll   U L l u

Ii   I L i l

EXTRA CREDIT! EXTRA CREDIT!

Are you in the headlines? Look at newspaper and magazine headlines and see how many letters of your name you can find. Circle each letter with a marker.

Alphabet and Beginning Sounds

Which is longer..5 years, 60 months, or 1826 days? Not any one! They are all the same!

How many crayons do you see?

Guess. ⬜ 3

Now count. ⬜ 9

How close was your guess?

What takes you longer, brushing your teeth or tying your shoes? Jumping ten times or tiptoeing across the room? Use a timer and test it out!

Estimating

Why did the elephant buy a bigger car?
He needed more trunk space.

Fill in the name tag.

Ask an adult if you need help with your address and telephone number.

Name **Christiana!!**

Address **Cummine**

Phone Number **77075 20830**

A person's initials are the first letters of the first, middle, and last name. What are your initials? What are the initials of the other people in your family? Are any of your initials the same?

Name, Address, Telephone Number

The Shape of Things

Knock Knock. Who's there?
You. You who?
Did you call?

Color the ▢s yellow

the ◯s blue

the △s red

the ▭s green.

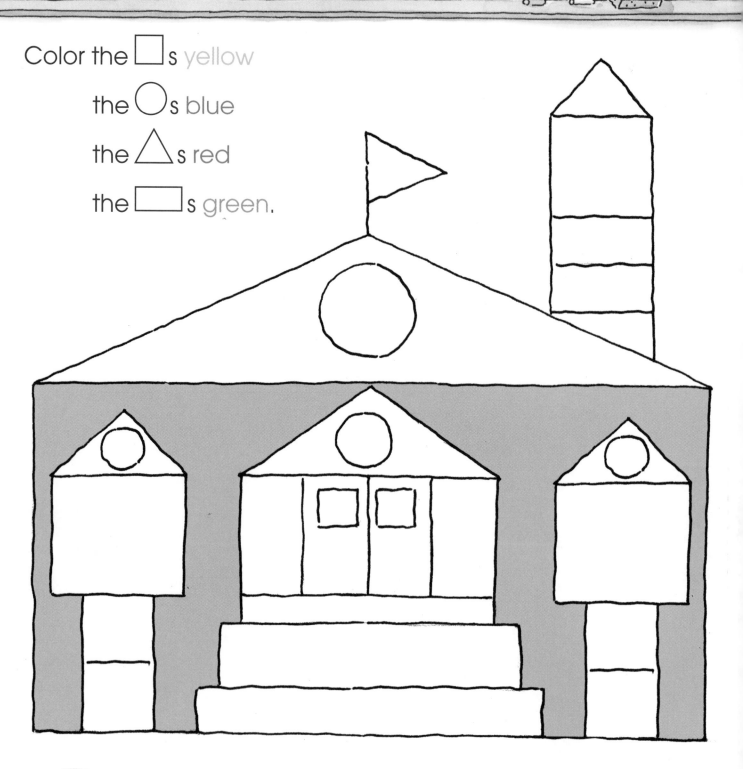

Make a shape exhibit! Go on a shape search in your home and look for objects that are square, round, triangular, or rectangular. Sort out objects into four groups and display them in a shape gallery.

Find the Opposite

Draw a line to match the opposites.

Can you think of opposite ways to move your body? Walk across the room in giant steps. Walk back with teeny-tiny steps. Tiptoe as quietly as you can. Then stamp loudly! What other opposites can you think of?

89

Opposites

There are 24 hours in every day.
There are 168 hours in every week.
There are 8736 hours in every year!

Is it morning, lunchtime, or night?

Draw a line to match each clock to its picture.

What time do you get up in the morning? What time do you go to bed at night? Draw pictures of digital clocks to show the times you do different things.

How Many?

Try saying this tongue twister three times in a row: Two timid toads talked.

How many of these can you find in the picture?

Count and write the number.

| 1 | 3 | 5 | 2 | 1 |

EXTRA CREDIT! Find something new to count! How many buttons are on your shirt? How many steps will it take you to get to the door?

©School Zone Publishing Company

91

Counting

A bike with 1 wheel is called a unicycle.
A bike with 2 wheels is called a bicycle.
A bike with 3 wheels is called a tricycle.

Look at the picture. Draw the missing parts.

Make up and tell a story
about the picture.

What's the weather like today? It's raining cats and dogs, and the streets are filled with poodles.

Number the pictures in 1, 2, 3 order.

 2

 3

1

Story Order

Amazing Bugs

Help each bug find its way to other bugs just like it.

EXTRA CREDIT! As you help the bugs find their way through the maze, make up stories about them!

Eye-Hand Coordination

Weather Watch

Thin feathery clouds are called cirrus clouds. They look like horses' tails! White puffy clouds are called cumulus clouds. They look like cotton balls.

Circle the picture that shows what you can do in different kinds of weather.

What's the weather like today? Is it warm? cold? windy? sunny? What does the sky look like? Make up a weather report and tell about today's weather.

95

Weather

Ice cream is a favorite food in America! Americans eat over a billion gallons of ice cream every year. That's about 24 quarts a year per person.

Draw a ☺ for what you like.

Draw a ☹ for what you don't like.

96

Likes and Dislikes

Here I Am!

Draw a picture of something you like to do in the summer.

Swing

Bike

What letter does your favorite summer activity start with? Can you think of a snack that starts with that letter? Can you think of a toy that starts with that letter? How many things can you do in an afternoon that start with that letter?

Drawing

Plan a picnic. Pick one food from each food group.

Draw it on the plate.

Make a recipe book! Draw pictures of some of your favorite snack foods. Think of the steps to make each snack. Ask an adult to help you make a list of the steps.

Row Your Boat

Circle the things in the bottom picture that are different.

Look at two pictures in a book. Try to find three things that are the same and three things that are different. Look at two pictures in two different books and try the same thing!

99

Same or Different

Family Gathering

How many families do you see?

Draw a line around each family.

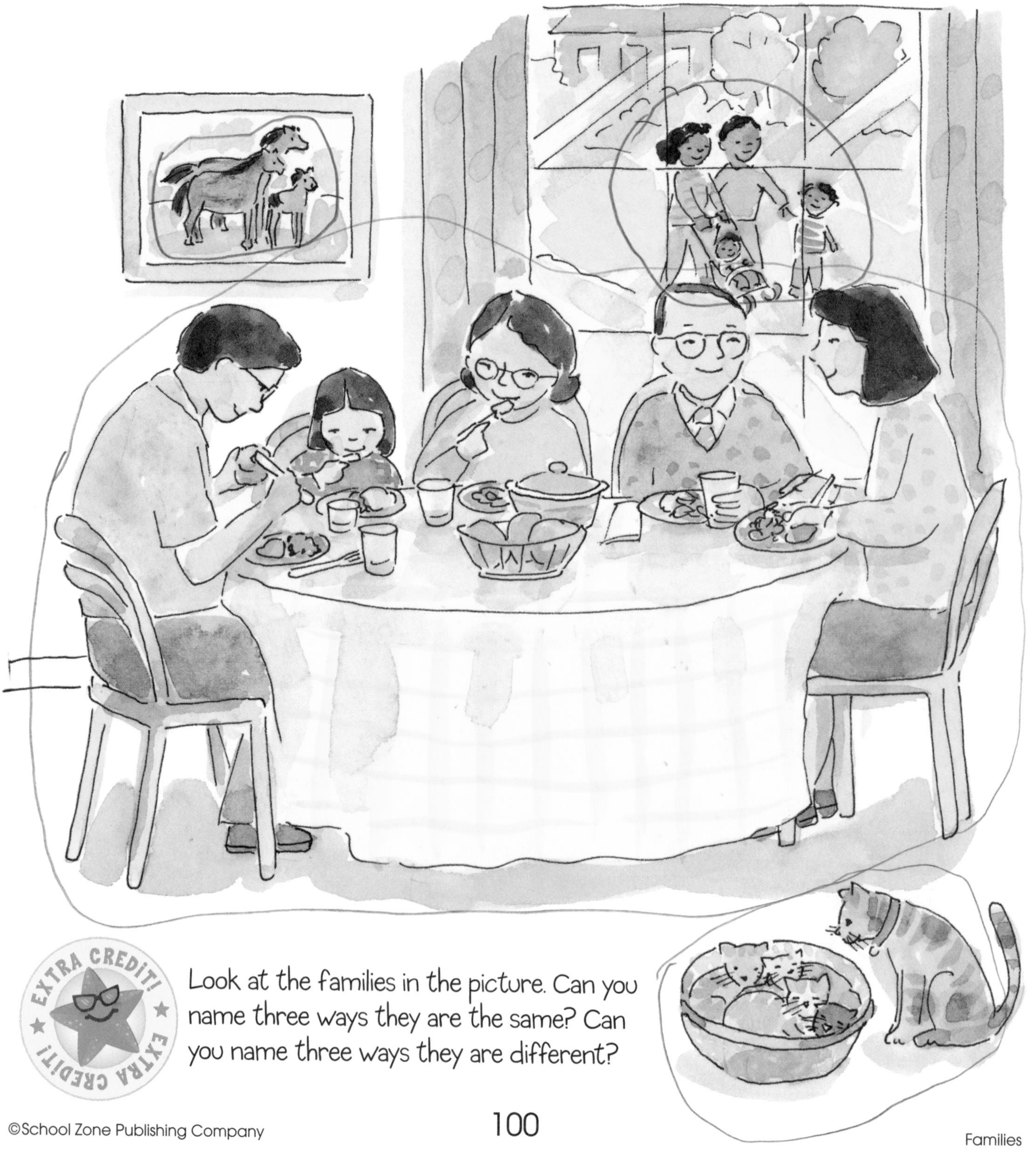

Look at the families in the picture. Can you name three ways they are the same? Can you name three ways they are different?

100

Families

People in the same family are called relatives.

Draw a picture of your family.

©School Zone Publishing Company

Families

Draw a line from each picture to its shadow.

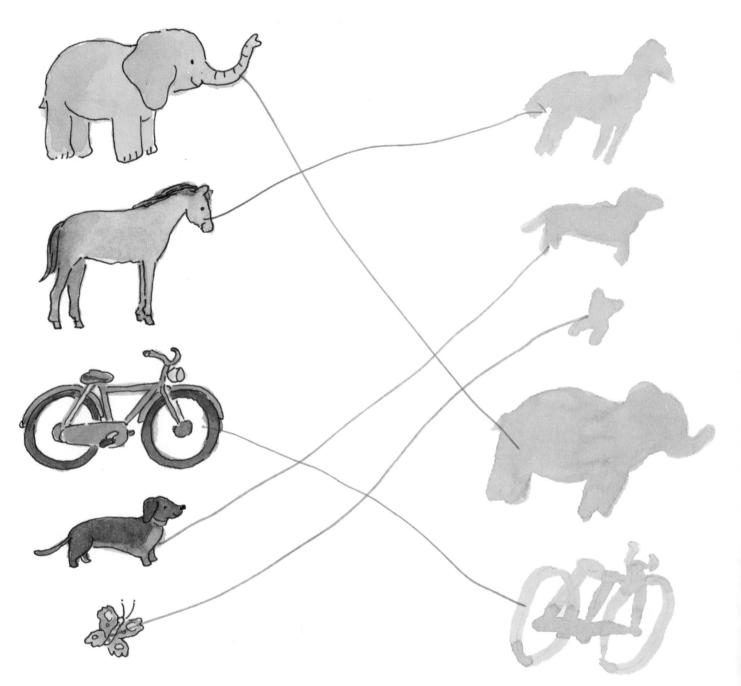

Take turns with a friend tracing each other's shadow. Use chalk outside on a sunny day. Retrace your shadows at the same place outside at different times during the day. What do you discover?

Put an **X** in the box to show who is following school rules.

	Follows rules	Doesn't follow rules
		X
		X
		X
	O	

EXTRA CREDIT! EXTRA CREDIT!

Ask an adult to help you make some instant pudding. Scoop some of the pudding onto a cookie sheet. Spread it around with a spatula. Then, with clean fingers, practice making letters. (You can lick your fingers in-between letters!)

Citizenship

Did you know that one strawberry has 200 seeds?

Draw a line from each food to what it is made from.

Ask an adult to help you make a summertime treat. For one serving of homemade ice cream, measure and mix together 1/2 cup whipping cream, 2 tablespoons powdered sugar, 1/2 teaspoon vanilla. Freeze. Then eat!

How many shoes does a centipede wear? None! A centipede doesn't wear shoes

Who belongs to each pair of shoes?

Draw a line to match.

How many things can you find that are the same size as your hand? Make a tracing of your hand. Then compare objects to see if they are longer or shorter than your hand.

105

Size Relationship

Circus Fun

Color the 🐢 green

the 🐱 yellow

the 🎩 blue

the ⬤ purple

the 👟 orange

the 🐦 red

the ⬭ brown

the 〰️ black

Color Words

EXTRA CREDIT! EXTRA CREDIT!

What colors are you wearing today?
Draw a picture to show.

Color Words

Summer Match-Ups

Knock Knock. Who's there?
Kent. Kent who?
Kent you come out and play with me?

Draw a line to show the things that go together.

Many objects are often used together in pairs. Some examples are salt and pepper, shoes and socks, and spoons and forks. Can you think of some more?

A Day at the Market

Look at the numbers in the picture.

$7.00/lb

$2.32

2 for $1.32

6 for 44¢

2 for 50¢

8 for 99¢

Booth 441

Booth 787

Booth 126

Booth 84

12 for $1.77

6/$1.50

2/50¢

19

How many of each number do you see? Fill in the chart.

zeros	ones	twos	threes	fours
5	7	8	2	5
fives	**sixes**	**sevens**	**eights**	**nines**
3	3	5	3	3

109

Number Recognition

Machines go click, clack, grrr, and boom. Machines go kerchunk, kerchunk, bang, and vroom!

Fill in the missing letters of the alphabet.

Alphabet Order

H   I   _   K   L

M

Q   _   O   N

X   _   Z

Perform a wheel test. Make a ramp by setting one end of a piece of
cardboard on a building block. Then roll different wheel toys from the top
of the ramp. Mark the place where each one stops rolling. Which rolled the
farthest? Are the results the same if you change the height of the ramp?

Activities to Share H_2O

BASIC SKILLS

Scavenger Hunt
> Make up and write a list of five to ten descriptions of things to look for on a walk. The list can contain items such as something rough, something round, something red, and something square. Then take a walk together and search for objects that fit the descriptions on the list.

What's Missing?
> Play a memory game together. Gather six common items and put them on a table. Ask your child to take a good look at the display and then close his or her eyes. Remove one item and then ask your child to look again and name the missing item. Then switch roles! Add more items to make the game more challenging.

Peeker Puzzle
> Cut a sheet of paper into horizontal strips so that one strip at a time can be peeled back. Lay the paper over a picture in a magazine or book. (Sticky notes can be used instead of paper strips.) Pull back the top strip and invite your child to guess what the whole picture might be. Then peel back the next strip and guess again!

Back-to-Back
> Gather crayons and paper. Sit back-to-back so that each person can only see his or her own paper. Pick one person to be the leader. The leader draws a picture and describes the colors and shapes being drawn at each step. The follower tries to make the same picture. When the pictures are complete, compare drawings. Then switch roles and try again!

I Spy
> Take turns describing something in the room or yard without telling what it is. Describe its size, its color, its shape, and any other attributes. Can the listener spy it, too?

Lemonade
> 3 lemons
> 3 tablespoons honey
> 3 cups water
> Measure honey and one cup of water into a pot. Stir over heat until honey is dissolved. Pour into a pitcher. Add two cups of cold water and the juice of three lemons. Chill and add ice.

MATH

Measuring with Yarn
> Demonstrate the long and short of measurement using yarn! Use the yarn to measure arms, legs, hands, and toes. Cut the yarn to show how long or short each part is. Make a measuring gallery and tape the yarn pieces up next to each other for comparison. Help your child make labels. Expand the activity to include other family members' measurements in the gallery!

Number Search
> Look for numbers together on a walk, in the house, or while out and about! Make a game out of finding one each of the numbers 1-10. Search together as a team or try to see who can find all ten numbers first (reporting each find along the way).

Shape Pictures

Cut out several big and small circles, squares, rectangles, and triangles in different colors of construction paper. Challenge your child to use the shapes to create a picture. Shapes can be glued onto a larger sheet of construction paper and details added to the picture with crayons or markers.

Counting All Around

Opportunities for counting abound. Make a game out of counting at odd moments, in between activities, on your way somewhere, or for a game all on its own. Ask number questions: "How many flowers do you see?" "How many birds can you count?" "Can you count how many forks?"

Car Graphing

Make a simple box graph for vehicle recording. Label the top row of boxes with different kinds of vehicles you might see: truck, bus, car, police car, motorcycle. Take the graph with you to a park or playground that has a street nearby for easy viewing. Then watch and record.

LANGUAGE ARTS

Share-a-Story

Read together! Read a favorite old story or a brand new book. Talk about the story as you read together. Ask questions: "What do you think will happen next?" "Why do you think he did that?" Encourage thinking: "What would you have done?" "How is the little pig in this book like the horse in the story we read yesterday?" "What do you think the horse would have done if he were in today's story?" Then visit your local library and help your child sign up for a library card!

Retell a Story

Choose a favorite story and retell it together. Take turns telling what happens next. Can you remember all the important parts? Read the story afterwards to check! (For a real challenge, try retelling a story together backwards! What was the last thing that happened in the story? What happened right before that? and before that?)

Grab-Bag Tales

Make up a story together! Use a grab bag of props for inspiration. Gather an assortment of common items such as a key, spoon, potato, rock, and ball of yarn and put them in a pillowcase. Grab an item out of the pillowcase at the beginning of each round and then find a way to add that item to the story!

Captions

Ask your child to tell you about a picture she has drawn. Write down her words exactly as she says them. Then read back the dictation to make sure the words are right! Display the picture along with the words. Read it again with your child later on.

Letter Books

Punch holes into the corners of index cards and loop them together with a paper ring (available at office supply stores). Choose one letter to start. Then search through old magazines for pictures that start with that letter. Pictures can be cut out and pasted on the cards.

Activities to Share

SOCIAL STUDIES

Make a Map
Create a map of the important places in your neighborhood. What's on your street? Take a walk around the neighborhood to check. Then paint, draw, or use blocks to map out what's there.

Family on Display
Cut out pictures of all the members of your family (including the dog and cat!) and tape the backs with strips of magnetic tape. Place on the refrigerator for both display and storytelling!

My Newspaper
On a large sheet of paper, write down and record the important news of the day. Follow the format of a newspaper, including a newspaper name, the date, and a weather report! Your child can invent a name for the newspaper and give the weather report. Then ask him to dictate sentences to tell about three important things that occurred during the day.

That's Me
Invite your child to paint a self-portrait—on a mirror! Add a little bit of liquid detergent to tempera paint. Your child can sit at a table with a hand mirror, observe closely, and paint just what she sees! When the painting is finished, make a print copy. Carefully place a sheet of white paper on top of the wet paint, smooth it down, and then peel it off.

SCIENCE

Surprise Seed
Dig up a cupful of dirt from a backyard, an empty lot, or a park and put it in a jar in a sunny window. Add enough water to moisten and then cover with a sandwich bag and seal with tape. The bag will create a greenhouse effect. Soon, any secret seeds hidden in the soil will begin to sprout and grow!

Ice Painting
Create an ice palette by adding a few drops of food coloring to water in an ice tray. Make several different colors and then freeze. When the ice is frozen, children can paint with it by sliding the ice cubes across a sheet of white paper. Encourage children to experiment with different colors. What happens when the colors meet?

Weather Watching
Observe and chart the weather each day for a month. Check outside each morning and make a picture symbol on a calendar to show whether it is sunny, rainy, cloudy, or windy. At the end of the month, count how many days of each kind of weather there were.

Natural Feels
Collect an assortment of pairs of natural objects (two leaves, two rocks, two pieces of bark, two twigs). Then challenge your child. Ask him to match the pairs while wearing a blindfold.

Activities to share

Basic Skills

Water Paint Get out paintbrushes and a bucket of water. Children can practice writing letters and numerals on the sidewalk or porch using brushes dipped in the water.

Ketchup Writing Pour a small amount of ketchup into a self-locking plastic bag. Lay the bag on a table and smooth it out to distribute the ketchup evenly. Children can write on the bag with their fingers and then smooth it over to start again.

Play Dough Mix together these ingredients to make dough that will keep for several days if stored in a covered container in a refrigerator.

> 2 cups flour
> 1 cup salt
> 1 cup water
> food coloring (optional)

Cooking with the Senses Cooking engages children's senses of taste, touch, sight, and smell. Cooking also teaches them to measure, plan, observe, and follow directions. Here are a couple of easy recipes for dishes you can make with your child.

Peanut Butter Milkshake

> 2 cups milk
> 1/3 cup creamy peanut butter
> 2 tablespoons honey
> Dash of cinnamon
> 4 ice cubes

Measure the first four ingredients into a blender. Blend for 10 seconds. Add ice cubes and blend again. Pour the shake into four glasses.

Saucy Grahams

> For each serving:
> 1 graham cracker
> 1/4 cup applesauce
> 2 tablespoons sweetened whipped topping

Place the graham cracker on a plate. Spread it with applesauce and garnish with a dollop of topping.

Memory Here's a memory game you can play at the supermarket. Before turning into the cereal aisle, ask children to think of three things pictured on the box of their favorite cereal. As you wheel down the aisle, challenge them to find the box. Look at the box together. Did they remember what was on it correctly? Or did they make a wild guess? Play the game again at another time, and they'll be sure to remember every detail.

Activities to share

Math

Shape Sandwiches Cut sliced cheese and bread into circles, squares, rectangles, and triangles for your child to identify. Once that's accomplished, he or she can match the shapes and build them into sandwiches.

Pasta Patterns Necklace String several kinds of hollow pasta, such as ziti, elbow macaroni, and rigatoni on waxed dental floss. Start with a simple pattern and have your child continue it. Children can use watercolors or markers to paint the necklace.

Two-Minute Drills Research suggests that the best way for children to learn math concepts is by manipulating objects, an easy and natural task to accomplish at home. Here are some simple, everyday things your child can do to gain experience using math concepts. You'll think of lots more.
- Estimate the number of peas on the plate; then count them.
- Count the blossoms on a plant.
- Check the temperature.
- Slice an orange in half. How many halves make a whole?
- Count the apples in a bowl. Share one with your child. How many are left?
- Estimate the number of bags you need to hold the leaves you've raked.
- Look at a clock to see if it's time for your favorite TV show.

If you're in a hurry, make a game of shopping. Engage your child in the race, and see if you can complete the shopping together in a specified time.

Language Arts

Cloud Stories Some sunny day, gather colored paper, white chalk, and a pen. Spread a blanket on the grass, lie on your back with your child, and watch the clouds. What do you see? Elephants? Giant footprints? Flowers? Talk about all the fantastic shapes you see. Your child can then make a chalk drawing of cloud shapes. When he or she is through, write the words your child dictates on the picture. To save the picture, spritz it with hairspray.

Reading Aloud It can't be said often enough: The best way to help your child become a reader is to read, read, read. Set aside a story time each day, perhaps before bed. Encourage your child to turn the pages and "read" aloud to you even if that means memorizing or making up the story. Point to words as you read them. Take delight in the story.

Activities to share

Science

Kitchen Science Set out two banana or apple slices. Dribble lemon juice on one. Leave the other plain. After a couple of hours, check the two pieces of fruit. What has happened to them? How has the one without lemon juice changed? Encourage your child to repeat the experiment with other fruits and vegetables. Ask whether all the fruits and vegetables reacted the way the apples and bananas did. How are the fruits and vegetables the same as the bananas or apples? How are they different?

Bug Recyclers After observing fruits and vegetables in the previous activity, put them outside on the ground. Take a look at them every day. Chances are you'll see bugs eating the fruits and vegetables or carrying bits away. They're doing their part to break down and recycle your garbage.

Social Studies

Keep on Trucking Watching trucks can be a lesson in economics. Just think of all the goods and people they carry! See if your child can identify what's in each one. Can he or she find a plumber's truck? An electrician's? A painter's? A landscaper's? Make truck hunting a part of your car or bus trips.

Safety Drill Teaching children what to do in an emergency builds their confidence—and yours, too. Make a fire escape plan and practice it. Be sure your child knows how to dial 911 and give his or her full name, telephone number, and address.

News of the Day From time to time, it's fun to review the events of the day with your child at bedtime. Where did your child go? What did he or she do? Who did he or she see? Expand the discussion to include plans for the next day and recollections of past events. Brief conversations like this help children understand past, present, and future, as well as develop oral language skills.

Recommended Reading

Books You'll Love Here are some books to tempt your kindergartner. They expand on the ideas and concepts presented in this book.

Barn Dance! by Bill Martin Jr. and John Archambault. There's a late-night party in the barn. Be there!

Bootsie Barker Bites by Barbara Bottner. Kids don't always get along!

Country Fair by Elisha Cooper; *Fair* by Ted Lewin. Two handsome books that follow children through their days at a fair.

Science Arts: Discovering Science Through Art Experiences by Mary Ann F. Kohl and Jean Potter. This book includes everything from ice sculptures to magic cabbage to entertain and educate your child.

The Empty Pot by Demi. A Chinese boy plants a seed in this touching fable.

How to Make an Apple Pie and See the World by Marjorie Priceman. Ingredients for an apple pie come from all around the world.

Little Bear Goes to Kindergarten by Jutta Langreuter and Vera Sobat. Little Bear learns that Mama leaves but also returns in this story translated from German.

My Little House ABC, adapted from the Little House books by Laura Ingalls Wilder. An easy-to-read adaptation from the classic series.

A Prairie Alphabet ABC by Yvette Moore. The seasons on a Canadian farm.

Read-Aloud Rhymes for the Very Young selected by Jack Prelutsky. An ever-popular book of lighthearted verse.

The Zebra-Riding Cowboy, A Folk Song from the Old West collected by Angela Shelf Medearis. An educated stranger proves he's not a greenhorn.

Recommended Reading

Here are some books to read and share together that expand on some of the themes in this book.

Chicka Chicka Boom Boom by John Archambault.
Colorful and lively chant about animated alphabet letters and a race up the coconut tree.

Counting Wildflowers by Bruce McMillan.
Beautiful, clear photographs introduce colors, counting, and flower names.

Famous Seaweed Soup by Antoinette Truglio Martin.
A modern-day beach adaptation of the story of the Little Red Hen.

Henry and Mudge in the Green Time by Cynthia Rylant.
Tales of the summer adventures of a boy and his dog.

I Got a Family by Melrose Cooper.
Exuberant, lively rhyming story about the joy of family.

I Grow, Too! by Karen Hoenecke.
A story that explores how animals and people change as they grow.

In the Small, Small Pond by Denise Fleming.
Rhythmic text introduces children to pond dwellers and their habits.

Jelly Beans for Sale by Bruce McMillan.
A bright and colorful concept book that introduces both coin values and simple addition.

Miss Bindergarten Gets Ready for Kindergarten by Joseph Slate.
Each letter of the alphabet is introduced in an entertaining rhyming tale about the first day of school.

My Five Senses by Aliki.
Clear, simple explanations describe the five senses and how to use them.

Popposites by Roger Culbertson.
A book full of pop-up pushes and pulls engagingly involves children in the exploration of opposites.

Stay Cool by Teresa Swenson.
A jungle adventure with vibrant illustrations.

Summer Legs by Anita Hakkinen.
Cheerful verse and tongue-twisting rhyme describes summer fun.

The Best Bug Parade by Stuart M. Murphy.
Size relationships are introduced as you follow this colorful bunch of bugs on parade

Zoo-Looking by Mem Fox.
The tale of Flora's day at the zoo.

Answers

Pages 2-3

Pages 4-5

Page 6

red
blue
yellow
green
orange
purple

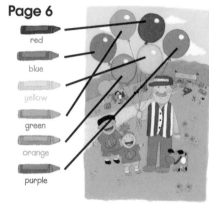

Page 7

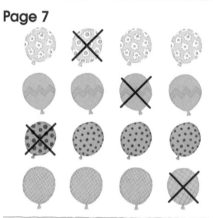

Page 8

1 ②(2) 3   1 2 ③(3)

①(1) 2 3   1 2 ③(3)

Page 9

Page 10

Page 11

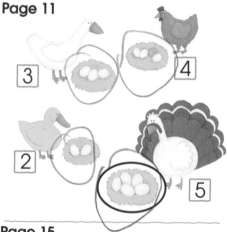

3   4

2   5

Pages 12-13

Children should have drawn mittens.

Page 14

Color pattern in the last row will vary but should be identifiable.

Page 15

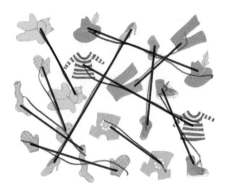

Answers

Page 16

The circles lead to the vegetables.

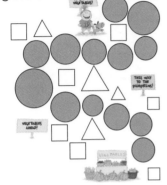

Page 19

A child should write his or her name, address, and telephone number.

Page 22

Page 23

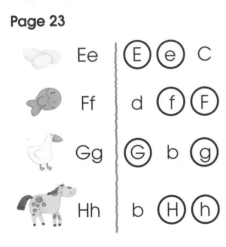

Ee   (E) (e) C

Ff   d (f) (F)

Gg   (G) b (g)

Hh   b (H) (h)

Page 17

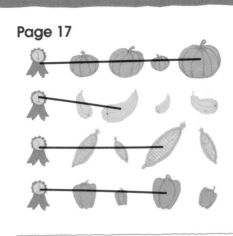

Page 20

Aa   (A) C (a)

Bb   (b) (B) A

Cc   a (c) (C)

Dd   (D) (d) C

Pages 24-25

7

6

8

6

Page 26

Favorite ride will vary.

6 people

Page 18

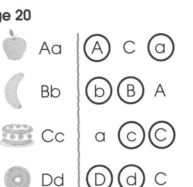

1   3   2

2   1   3

Page 21

How many 🍐s?   3   6   2   (4)

How many 🍌s?   (7)   4   3   5

How many 🍊s?   (6)   3   5   7

How many 🍎s?   4   6   2   (5)

Page 27

Answers will vary.

121

Answers

Page 28
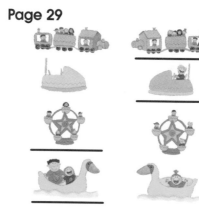

down — off
top — up
full
empty
on — bottom

Page 29

Page 30

Page 31
Drawing should include one food from each of the four groups.

Page 32

Ii — (I) (i) e
Jj — d (j) (J)
Kk — (k) b (K)
Ll — (l) c (L)
Mm — (M) (m) a
Nn — f (N) (n)

Page 33

Plastic   Metal   Paper

Page 34

1¢   5¢   10¢   25¢

Page 35

Oo — (O) c (o)
Pp — (p) (P) d
Qq — i (Q) (q)
Rr — n (r) (R)
Ss — (s) n (S)
Tt — (T) L (t)

Page 36
Row 1: Cat, hat, and bat should be colored.

Row 2: Chair, bear, and pear should be colored.

Row 3: Coat, goat, and boat should be colored.

Row 4: Fan, can, and pan should be colored.

Page 37
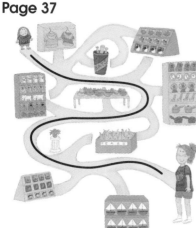

Page 38
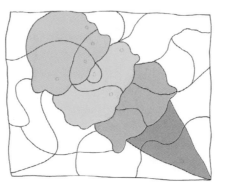

Page 39
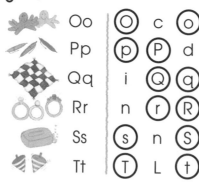

1 2 (3) 4 5
1 2 3 (4) 5
1 (2) 3 4 5
1 2 3 4 (5)

Ice cream should be colored in.

Answers

Pages 40-41

1. 3
2. 2
3. 4
4. 3
5. 3

Pages 44-45

The **roller coaster** is the most popular ride at the fair.

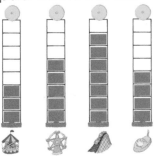

Page 48

Children should draw the other half of the clown.

Page 49

1. 7
2. 5½
3. 6½
4. 4½

Page 52

Page 56

Drawing will vary.

Page 42

Page 43

Page 46

Page 47

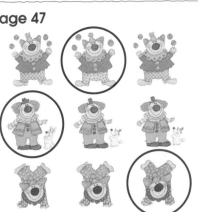

Page 50

Page 51

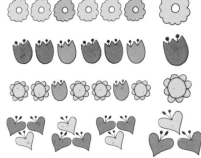

Page 53

Pages 54-55

Answers

Answers

Page 58

There are 5 silly things.

Page 59

Page 60

Page 61

Pages 62-63

Page 64

Page 65

Page 66

Answers

Page 67

There are 9 things that start with b.

Page 68

Aa 🍎
Kk 🪁
Mm 🐭
Pp 🍐
Rr 🐰
Tt 🐢

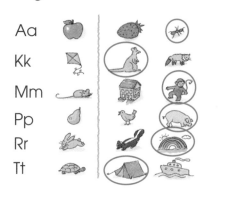

Page 69

1. 4
2. 3
3. 1

Page 70

Page 71

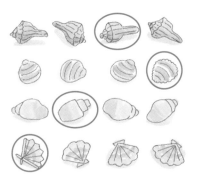

Page 72

Page 73

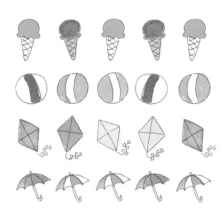

Page 74

Children should draw a picture of what happens next. Picture will vary.

Page 75

Answers

Page 76

Page 77

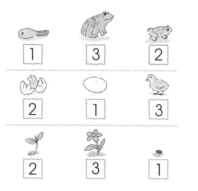

Page 78

frogs		④	1	3
ducks		6	⑤	4
mice		③	4	2
butterflies		2	5	④
children		3	⑥	5

Page 79

Page 80

Page 81

Page 82

Answers will vary.

Page 83

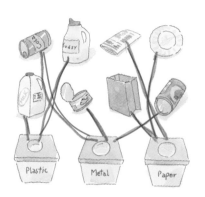

Page 85

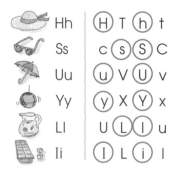

Page 86

9 crayons

Page 87

Answers will vary.

Page 84

Page 88

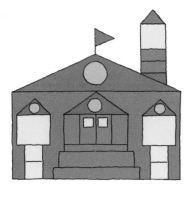

Page 89

Page 90

Page 91

Page 92

Page 93

Page 94

Other pathways that work are acceptable.

Page 95

Pages 96-98

Answers will vary.

Page 99

Answers

Page 100

Page 101
Answers will vary.

Page 102

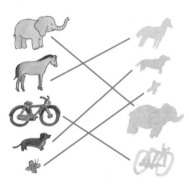

Page 104

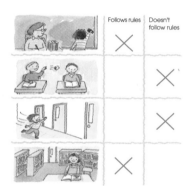

Page 103

	Follows rules	Doesn't follow rules
	X	
		X
		X
	X	

Page 105

Page 106-107
Check colored picture.

Page 109

zeros	ones	twos	threes	fours
5	7	8	2	5
fives	sixes	sevens	eights	nines
3	3	5	3	3

Page 108

Pages 110-111

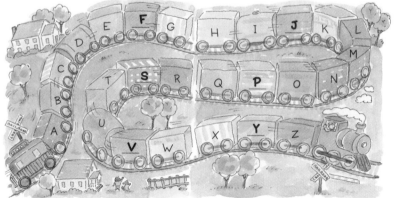

Kindergarten Scholar 02457